Making your GOALS
First Class

*Five principals you need to know
to succeed at your Goals*

ERVIN GOODE

ISBN: 978-1-4669-3604-1 (sc)
ISBN: 978-1-4669-3605-8 (e)

Trafford rev. 03/13/2014

 www.trafford.com

North America & international
toll-free: 1 888 232 4444 (USA & Canada)
fax: 812 355 4082

This book is dedicated to the crew.

I love you all. Thanks for your support.

Contents

Preface

I was born ten days before Valentine's Day in 1960, an era when our society was trying to live together like God intended. On February 4, wrapped up in a light blue blanket, I looked like a sweet piece of chocolate Valentine's candy ready to show my love and respect for being alive. I approached life cautiously and quietly, working hard at whatever I tried to do. Even through elementary, middle, and high school, I believed that living simply and enjoying the love of friends and family was the only way to live. I was fortunate to fall in love with my high school sweetheart. We got married shortly after high school, and a baby boy came along later. We were truly happy and blessed.

I found out quickly that life was not going be a bed of roses. My wife and I decided to end our marriage and go our separate ways. Having a son to take care of was a wonderful task to have. I was approach by a gentleman about a job interview for a Fortune 500 company in the oil and gas industry. I fell in love with Shell Oil Company, its culture, and the yellow Shell pectin. Shell Oil management launched me into the supervisor development program to development my leadership and interpersonal skills. I worked in four different states. I have met hundreds of different people along my journey with Shell Oil Company.

During the month of February, people begin to think of love and romance, but it was in the month of May when I met my wife and her lonely and wonderful children. I fell in love with her and her kids. I am grateful to have three kids to call my own.

When you read any book that I have written, the word of God will be in the first paragraph or chapter. He is the only source from which my help and protection come. I have belonged to many churches during my travels and listened to different pastors and preachers. The one who stands out is Pastor Baines of Macedonia Baptist Church in Dayton, Ohio.

I recognized that all people need help all over this world, so I started looking for ways to help people in need. I joined the Texas Prisons System Ministry to help the inmates develop certain skills that they would need before being released back into sociality. Unfortunately, I did not get involved like I had planned. I continue to seek organizations and programs that I can use to help develop myself into the person

God wants me to be. I joined the Toastmaster Organization to improve my public speaking and leadership skills.

The month of February is the shortest month on the calendar, typically twenty-eight days; however, I was born on the fourth day of the month, which left me twenty-four days until the end of the month. These remaining twenty-four days remind me of twenty-four hours that we have each day. I try to make each hour of the day that I am awake count for something positive.

There were so many topics to write on, which made this book a challenge. So I decided to write about something that made me happy and brought me joy. In addition, I had fun doing it. I hoped it would not take very long to write what I consider a special self-awareness and powerful book once I made up my mind to share these principles of success with the public. The reality is it took several years to pen down what I knew worked.

For as long as I can remember, I have written things down—things that I found interesting, my thoughts, and my feeling about issues that I did not want to forget. So writing a book was in my DNA early on.

It is sad to see and hear that people are bored with life. It is also equally disappointing to find people searching to find their purpose in life only to later give up to drugs or crime. I believe this book will help motivate and rejuvenate anyone who truly needs a positive change in his or her life.

These principles are more powerful than an F5 tornado when they work together. Read each chapter, keeping in mind the main topic. At the end of each chapter, jot down some notes, ideas, or thoughts under the topics that you just read about. By the time you get to the end of the book, there will be a personal road map to aid you on your exciting journey.

Introduction

I sat in an assigned seat on a Continental Learjet on a cold October morning as we waited our turn to position ourselves and get permission from the airport controller to take off. Looking out through the thick, insulated, double-panel glass, I could see snow flurries falling gently on the wings of the plane that was waiting so patiently.

My focus changed when the pilot announced that we could finally begin takeoff. The jet started slowly moving down the long, concrete runway. The plane began to gradually pick up speed and then began to slow back down without any warning. Suddenly, the plane exited the runway and headed back toward the terminal.

Looking around the cabin of the plane at the faces of the passengers and flight attendants, you could tell that something was wrong, but we did not know what it was. Then the mystery question that was on everyone's mind was answered when the captain announced he wanted to make sure the plane was completely deiced before we took off. He apologized for the inconvenience, but he wanted to make sure that our trip was as safe and enjoyable as possible.

After the Continental Airline's crew finished deicing the midsized jet, they gave the captain the okay to leave the deicing area. The airplane captain worked his way back into the airplane takeoff lineup, so we could get our chance to take off again.

Our destination was Houston, Texas, and the flight time was scheduled for about two hours. We were ready to take off. The jet raced down the runway and then slowly started to lift into the air, cutting through the snow flurries that were falling from the sky. The plane began to climb to the altitude that cleared the control tower. There were so many planes coming in and taking off that the air traffic controller had to map a safe path out of the airspace of the airport. As we maneuvered our way out of the airport airspace, the plane began to level off and the flight attendants started to move around inside the fuselage.

It seems that the pilot and plane found the perfect airspace. The pilot set the computer toward Houston, Texas, and called ahead for the current weather conditions, wind speed, and temperature.

My concentration was once again broken by the pilot. "I am turning off the seat belt sign, and I want to update you on the current weather conditions in Houston."

Two hours later we landed in Houston Intercontinental Airport. There was a significant difference in the temperature when you compared Ohio and Texas—thirty-eight degrees in Dayton, Ohio, and sixty-five degrees in Houston, Texas. It was nice to be back in my home state, but I kept flashing back to the plane preparing to take off and then suddenly being forced to divert because of some unexpected problems. It is so much like life's unexpected problems. Just when you think you have everything under control, something unexpected comes along that takes us off track.

The approach to winning is to find a way to keep your mind and focus on the runway until you take off. My definition of *Takeoff* is defined is having the mental awareness to spring forward to grasp the opportunities that suddenly appear in our life. In this book, I will show you what it would take to stay focused on the path to your dreams. These success principals are based on a plane flight using termlogy from air travel, but the message is clear: your dreams and goals can be achieved if you simply believe and commit yourself to using the principles in this book and recognizing that God is the pilot of your live.

I will show you steps and specific methods that you can use immediately. This book has taken into account different events, so we can keep flying in the right direction at all times. Using the five success principles of focus, faith, flexibility, follow-through, and fun will allow you to keep your compass pointing in the right direction at all times. Each principle will be fully explained in the chapters to follow.

Chapter 1

If you stay focused and stay on track, you will get to where you want to be.

—Michelle C. Ustaszeski

Principle 1: Focus

Focus on the Right Destination

B eing successful in life is not guaranteed. It is easier to fail than to succeed. Take the gifted professional athletes who make a lot of money playing sports, wealthy preachers, successful lawyers, influential mayors, and company presidents who sometimes lose their focus and find themselves in scandals, locked up in prison, or dead.

It always amazes and disappoints me when I hear about athletes who were worth millions of dollars and later in their careers find themselves financially broke and struggling to get by. Jim Rohn once said, "Failure is not a single, cataclysmic event. You don't fail overnight. Instead, failure is a few errors in judgment, repeated every day."

It is easy to get off course trying to pursue our desired destinations or goals by making those little, insignificant errors in judgment every day until we find ourselves so far off course we just don't know how we wound up there. If you get the right flight ticket, you can always check to see where you should be going. Your goals are like flight tickets to keep you focused on your main destination. Your focus, or goal, should be clearly mapped out on a course that is comprehensible and very distinct. Referring back to your flight ticket from time to time allows you to stay focused on your goal. These properly prepared flight tickets are the road maps for your goals. They will let you know where you are going. Well, you may ask, how do I know that I have the right ticket or am pursuing a worthy goal?

Know Your Destination

As we pursue our lifelong endeavourers, whatever they are, here is the secret you need to know: the first step is to know what you want. Next, you will determine how long it will take to accomplish it. There are two types of goals that you to need to focus on: long-term and short-term goals, and they should be smart goals. Smart goals are goals that are specific, measurable, attainable, realistic, and time-sensitive. Sometimes you find people with short- and long-range goals linked together; in a sense, it's like having connecting flights to get to your final destination. There is nothing wrong with having both short- and long-range goals. In fact, in some cases, it is the right thing to do. I would like to focus on long-range goals.

You must have a clear goal, a planned destination. If you don't know the airport you want to land at, it doesn't matter which flight you take; you will not get there. As you began to put the necessary energy and time in to developing and focusing on your goals, be open-minded to the fact that everything is possible.

If you begin to wonder where you should start, let me give you a good starting point. Most people have a passion for something that they love to do or a special skill that has put them above the average person. For example, you may be good at public speaking, teaching, or taking care of other people. Here are some suggestions to get you thinking: What do you read about for hours when you are bored? Is there something you find yourself researching to learn more about? Is there something you loved to do as a child but have abandoned because you got older? Do you have a hobby that you are currently doing on the side that could be turned into a full-time business?

You should also look around your room to see what items you find yourself collecting. This could give you clues to some hidden passion. Always keep your mind open, so you can focus on that little passion that pops up from time to time. Try to remember the times when you had a strong desire to do something positive or rewarding to make people's lives easier or better. Put a little time and effort into developing this thought. It just may be of some value to everyone. In most cases, these passions and desires you have could be worth pursuing in life.

I heard a wonderful story, which I believe will prove my point about pursuing your internal, burning passion.

An elementary school teacher was giving a drawing class to a group of six-year-old children. At the back of the classroom sat a little girl who normally did not pay much attention in school. In the drawing class, she did.

For more than twenty minutes, the girl sat with her arms curled around her paper, totally absorbed in what she was doing. The teacher found this fascinating. Eventually, she asked the girl what she was drawing. Without looking up, the girl said, "I'm drawing a picture of God."

Surprised, the teacher said, "But nobody knows what God looks like."

The girl said, "They will in a minute."

Consider these points to help validate you desires:

- Ensure the desire is legal and not life threatening; then it would be worth pursuing.
- Make sure your purpose helps more people than just yourself.
- Pray about this burning desire and ask the question: would this help someone to change his life in a positive way?

Finding this right goal to focus on is not easy, so before you purchase a ticket for the journey, be sure you are certain. Sometimes the hardest step to make toward any process is the first step.

Staying focused on your goal or main mission is like taking a vacation. The first things you should do is get prepared for the vacation. Once the destination and departure date are known, you shift into preparation mode. Start preparing yourself immediately for your new goal or position.

For example, let's say that you want to win a marathon. You would start focusing on getting in condition for a race. You would prepare yourself to eat right and make sure you have the best running gear, including running shoes and sweats. A good runner knows that it is important to know the terrain and the possible weather conditions during the race, so it's important to practice in similar conditions.

Keep in mind that this is all about staying focused on what you are trying to achieve. It is important to be prepared for the target you are aiming at, because once you hit it, you should be ready to step right in. You may have had a dream to be a commercial airplane pilot for a major airline. I would tell you this: if your passion is to fly planes, go for it. But start preparing to be a commercial pilot. Work on your people skills while you train. Then, once you reach your milestone as a pilot, you will be better suited for the job, because you have been preparing for it.

Here is the point: all this preparing is a good way to keep focused on the target. Sometimes the preparation is frustrating, because you find yourself sacrificing a lot of your time from friends and family to pursue your goal. Those individuals who are willing to focus on their goals and prepare themselves mentally and physically will surely reach them.

Look at Tiger Woods' early childhood. We all know that Tiger Woods is a gifted and passionate professional golfer; there is no argument about that. But it was his father's love and observation that recognized his talent. If it were not for his father's focus and personal drive to help prepare his young son, Tiger Woods would probably not be the golfer that he is today. In Tiger's case, he is always preparing himself for the match.

Here are a few thoughts worth remembering:

- What is your passion (hobbies and things you enjoy doing)?
- If you can see it, if you believe you can, it will happen.
- Take the time to prepare and be ready to perform when you reach your goal.

Focus on Your Goal

Write your main goal at the bottom of this chart and then list the steps it will take to reach this milestone at the beginning of this chart.

Steps to Reach Your Goal

1.

2.

3.

4.

5.

Steps to Reach Your Secondary Goal

1.

2.

3.

4.

5.

Short-Range Goal Target Date: _____

Long-Rage Goal Target Date: _____

Chapter 2

Believe in yourself! Have faith in your abilities! Without a humble but reasonable confidence in your own powers you cannot be successful or happy.

—Norman Vincent Peale

Principle 2: Faith

There is a higher being, a force that protects us, guides us, and loves us. I would admit that I'm in no way deserving of that unconditional love; however, I do believe that this force exists. Sometimes our actions may show something different; otherwise, I have to admit that believing in this invisible but powerful force is real. On the other hand, when it comes to believing in ourselves, it is a different story. My faith is strong when it comes to these different beliefs. I define faith in this section as the substance of things hoped for and the evidence of things not seen.

When I boarded the plane for the flight from Dayton to Houston, I had faith that I would make it to Houston. But when the plane suddenly veered off of the runway to go through another deicing process before taking off, my faith dropped for only a second. For only a second I lost faith in the plane's ability to safely fly, the pilots' ability to control and steer the plane, and the weather's ability to stay as it was and not get any worst. But my lack of faith lasted for only for a minute, because my focus was on going to Houston and I was committed to stay the course.

You can read many books on faith. The Bible would be the best to read, in my opinion. They would all say something similar in nature; however, I strongly believe that having this unshakable faith is a very important step on your journey to being successful. Let's say that you must master this little five-letter word. You must learn to: trust it, believe it, live it, and never doubt it.

It's important to understand all the forces that come into play when you have unwavering faith. If you can stay focused and have faith, then you will know and believe that you can conquer your problems and overcome any adversity that you may encounter. Taking on any task that you have set your mind to allows you to approach those challenges with a difference mind-set.

The Bible tells us in Matthew 17:20 that if we have faith like a mustard seed, we will be able to move mountains. I believe this to be true. Sometimes our problems seem like mountains, and sometimes people give up too soon. They lose the faith.

When you decide to go for something, really focusing on it shows that you are 100 percent committed. You need to work on staying faithful to your goal or, in my case, destination. When things start to look like everything is getting out of control and you began to doubt yourself, please hold on to your faith. You must take the time to reflect back to a time when you found yourself in a situation where you had no control and somehow you made it though. Those are the times when you kept the faith.

It's like having the confidence knowing that you will reach your destination even if you have to detour through a couple of different cities to get to where you are going. So in those times when you feel grounded, remember the successes you had before. This will let you know that you can do it.

Learn to have faith in the things and people around you. Sometimes God puts the right pilots in place to fly your plane for you, someone to protect you and guide you along your journey. Sometimes the situations that you are going through seem hopeless, and then someone or something comes along and helps change your situation for the positive.

I would have to admit that I get a little nervous at high elevations, and for a long time I was scare to fly. I had enough fear about looking out the window of a tall building or flying that I tried to avoid those situations whenever I could. When we lose faith, we allow fear to move into our thought processes and destroy our dreams and goals.

So let me make it clear. There are two types of fear we deal with. The fear that exists in our minds and the fear that is real and tangible. If you allow yourself to listen to the fear in your mind, it will find a way to slowly destroy your self-esteem and ultimately your will to pursue you dreams. The best way to deal with this type of fear is to bring it out of the darkness of your mind and into the light. In other words, deal with it or get help to conquer it. Having the fear in your mind that you will fail at something before you've even had the chance to try it is a example of letting fear and worry control you.

Dealing with fear that is real, life-threatening, or frightening is totally a different subject. For example, being threatened by someone pointing a handgun at you is something to be concerned about. So when I talk about fear in this chapter, just remember that I am referring to the fear in the mind not the physical or threatening.

I am reminded of a Bible story about three young men who looked fear dead in the eye and knew faith was backing them up. I'm referring to the story of Shadrach, Meshach, and Abed-Nego as told in Daniel 3:13-30.

King Nebuchadnezzar gave orders to bring Shadrach, Meshach, and Abed-Nego before him so he could asked them if it was true that they did not worship or serve his golden god. The king told them that he was going to give them a second chance, and if they didn't fall down and worship the statue he'd made, they would be thrown into the furnace of blazing fire. The three told the king that they didn't need to give him an answer. They knew that if the God they worshiped existed, he would save them if he willed it, so they wouldn't fall down and worship the king's statue. This really made the king mad; not only did his facial expression changed, but his rage increased to a point that he ordered the furnace to be heated seven times higher than normal. The three young men were tied up fully dressed and thrown into the furnace.

Just imagine for a second these three guys standing there, watching the furnace being heated seven times hotter than normal and knowing that they are going to be cremated. If they were going to fear something, this would be a good time. They didn't lose their faith; they didn't say "Wait a minute. We were just joking" or "Hold on a second. We are going to worship your statue." Starring fear in the face is not easy. It takes faith.

Remember that when it seems like your dreams and goals are slipping away, it's important to not give up. Keep pressing on. That's why it's so important to have your goals written down. It allows you to have something you can see in writing.

Well, you know how the story ends. Shadrach, Meshach, and Abed-Nego were not harmed at all while they were inside the furnace. Only the ropes that bound their hands and feet were burned off, and miraculously, there was a fourth person in the furnace with them. This blew King Nebuchadnezzar's mind to the point that he had to knowledge that the God that Shadrach, Meshach, and Abed-Nego worshipped must be acknowledged and respected.

This story should bring home how important it is to have faith and not let fear cripple you. Maintaining your faith in what you are doing is not going to be easy. When you find yourself losing your faith, focus on your goal again. If you get excited about the journey you are on, you will feel the desires and the emotions, plus your faith will began to reemerge.

Focus on Your Goal

Write your main goals at the bottom of this chart and then list the steps it will take to reach this milestone at the beginning of this chart.

Steps to Reach Your Goal

1.

2.

3.

4.

5.

Steps to Reach Your Secondary Goal

1.

2.

3.

4.

5.

Short-Rage Goal Target Date: _____

Long-Range Goal Target Date: _____

Chapter 3

We can never be certain about the future and therefore we must continue to be flexible and adaptable so that we can react quickly to the needs of our clients and our market place.

—Talal Abu-Ghazaleh

Principle 3: Be Flexible

Planes do not fly very well with ice covering their wings and fuselage. In 2010, there were total 828 fatalities in several different plane crashes in the United States. Equipment has been destroyed and lives have been lost in airplane crashes. Nevertheless, every day you can see or hear a plane in the sky. This is still the safest way to travel; there is not a doubt in my mind.

When you focus on your goals or your destination with faith, you will find a way to see it through. And having the wisdom to change if you need to is priceless. Having the courage to be flexible allows you to make things better. It frees you up and allows you to look at different options. You may wonder how being flexible makes some thing better. For example, having our trip to Houston interrupted because the pilot felt the plane needed to be deiced again only made the flight possible and safer, so no one had a problem with it. We were flexible with our departure time. Getting there safely outweighed the risk of flying with extra weight. We felt good about the flight.

Sometimes you spend a lot of time mapping out life's master plan only to find yourself in a storm of trouble that threatens that plan. You should not give up. When you try to analyze why this happens, you could become discouraged. Be flexible to adapt to the sudden change and find new ways to overcome your adversity.

Some people make the mistake of thinking that what they are doing must work, and they spend their money trying to prove to themselves and others that their plan is well thought out. Even when it's clear it's not working, they find themselves recalculating and pondering over why the plan is not working but refuse to change something to the plan so it would have a better chance of succeeding. If this is the case in your life, you may need to take another look at your situation. It may be that the conditions have changed and you need to be a little flexible to get things back on track again. Let's be clear on the definition of flexible in this section. Being *flexible* means having the ability to be able to adjust to change and being adaptable when situations change.

The following story is an example of this.

When Mike was in is midforties, he began a job as a welder for a Fortune 500 oil and gas company. He realized that his skill was a very valuable commodity. He realized that if he could hire a few people and start his own company, he could really make a difference in his life.

After several years of working as contractor for this company he decided to go into business on his own. He turned down offers from people who wanted to hire him. He ignored the people who tried to scare him by warning him about failing and losing lots of money. He decided to stay with this idea of starting his own company.

I believe that if Mike would have listened to the negative forces of his friends and relatives and not had the courage to step out in faith, Sonntag Lease Service wouldn't be a reality today. This example is more about adapting to those unforeseen forces that try to destroy your dreams. The future is unpredictable, and the world is unfair at times. You need to be able to take a little pain with the joy, but whatever you do, do not take your eyes off your goal. Stay flexible and have a backup plan.

Focus on Your Goal

Write your main goal at the bottom of this chart and then list the steps it will take to reach this milestone at the beginning of this chart.

Steps to Reach Your Goal

1.

2.

3.

4.

5.

Steps to Reach Your Secondary Goal

1.

2.

3.

4.

5.

Short-Range Goal Target Date: _____

Long-Range Goal Target Date: _____

Chapter 4

It was character that got you out of bed, commitment that moved us into action, and discipline that enabled us to follow through.

—Zig Ziglar

Principle 4: Follow Through

When a plane is on the runway at speeds of two hundred miles per hour and the wheels just begin to leave the ground, this is the point that pilots call the point of no return. The pilot gives a final thrust, allowing the aircraft to propel into the air.

As a passenger, you can feel the g-force on your body. The plane begins to climb into the airspace that the air traffic controller has picked out to ensure the safest altitude to fly. When you compare this analogy to your dreams and goals, you should not take it lightly.

Your dreams and goals are important to keep on the radar screen in you mind. Yes, there will be setbacks and disappointments along the way, but until you reach your goal, you must continue to follow through.

The definition of *follow through* in this chapter is the act of proceeding with a task to the end. Giving up is not an option.

This may be the most important step to consider, because this step could be the one to make or break you. It is a mistake to work so hard on something and then give up. Sometimes people come up just shy of succeeding. To follow through on a worthily goal takes a unique character, commitment, action, and discipline. We can explore each of these success ingredients.

Character

Character is defined here as having a determined attitude and remarkable behavior that displays excellence and integrity about oneself.

In most cases, when a person experiences something horrible, it plays a major part in shaping that person's mental attitude as well as his belief and philosophy of who he really is. One way to begin to develop the right character for success is to believe in yourself. This sounds simple, and you have probably heard this statement uttered by many different people. Motivational speakers, coaches, even your parents have most likely used it at some point in time. Guess what? They are right.

Here is one example of why they are right. Examine the attitude and behavior of an airplane's flight attendants during a rough flight. As the plane is being bumped around due to severe turbulence, they try to remain calm and reassuring for the passengers. We know they are pretending to be fearless, despite the fact that they are thinking the same thing as the passengers. If you could take a flight every day and experience the most severe turbulence on every flight, I believe that you would start to develop a mind-set of not worrying.

Worrying about something you have no control over is a waste of time. In fact, it often takes your focus away from what is important to the degree that you fail. So don't lose your focus. The conditions seem, bad but things are going to be okay.

To develop this unique character, you must be determined to win and possess an attitude that refuses to quit. You must continue to follow though regardless of the turbulence that you may encounter.

Commitment

Commitment means different things to different people. Here is the definition: having a convincing attitude that you will never quit something and that you start regardless of what happens. In this day and time, it is easier to fail than to succeed. In most cases, people simply give up, giving into the obstacles they encounter. Making a commitment is like getting married to your high school sweetheart.

My Uncle Willie and his wife Mar Rose have been married for forty-five years, and they have four children—three girls and one boy. At a family reunion, I had an opportunity to talk to him about the commitment he made to his wife some forty-five years ago. He said that his love for her was unbreakable, but as time passed on and they found themselves working two jobs and having children, they noticed that they argued more, didn't speak to each other at times, and even thought about leaving each other at one time. He said he just wanted to give up; however, there came a turning point in their lives when he realized that his commitment to his wife was more important than just giving up. Unfortunately, they lost one daughter years ago. Their surviving children are now grown up and living their own lives. He and his wife have plenty of grandchildren to occupy their time. He currently suffers with a touch of Alzheimer's, but he is still committed to his marriage.

When you are truly committed to something, giving up is not an option. Do your research and know your options, so you can make the most intelligent decisions about your endeavor.

Having all the details of the possible rewards and benefits, plus knowing the consequences if something were to go wrong with your endeavor, makes it somewhat easy to commit. Looking back over your life, you can see how well you have navigated around the pitfalls.

Action

Everything we desire in life that we commit to will take some action from us to make it a reality. Action is defined as the processes of doing or acting in a way that the follow-through process keeps your focus on your goals. Where there is no action or energy exerted toward a task or goal the goal will have a hard time becoming a reality.

Let's face it. You have to make some effort if you want anything in life or want to see if the if the craziest idea you have in your head will really work. Take the story of the Wright brothers, who had the crazy idea of flying aircraft. On December 17, 1903, Orville Wright piloted the first powered airplane twenty feet above the ground in North Carolina. That event forever changed the course of history. After conceiving this notion, they began to put this concept into action by experimenting in 1896 at their bicycle shop in Dayton, Ohio. You have to be willing to do the work.

Discipline

From my prospective, one of the hardest ingredients when following through is to train yourself to be disciplined enough to ignore the things that don't matter and always pursue the things that do.

Let's define discipline. Discipline is having the mental faculties to have self-control and obedience over oneself to follow through on tasks. As you write you goals down, this becomes a very important step in your success; however, the steps to get there are also very important. You must have the self-control to train yourself to follow those steps, give yourself time to work the steps, and discipline yourself to follow though.

Focus on Your Goal

Write your main goal at the bottom of this chart and then
list the steps it will take to reach this milestone at the
beginning of this chart.

Steps to Reach Your Goal

    1.

    2.

    3.

    4.

    5.

Steps to Reach Your Secondary Goal

    1.

    2.

    3.

    4.

    5.

Short-Range Goal Target Date: _____

Long-Range Goal Target Date: _____

Chapter 5

People rarely succeed unless they have fun in what they are doing.

—Dale Carnegie

Principle 5: Have Fun

In this final chapter, I want to list the success principle that I call *fun*. The word *fun* is defined in the *Macmillan Dictionary* as amusement or enjoyment. Throughout this chapter when the word *fun* is mention, it will have the meaning of having joy. It seems to me that if a person's attitude is positive, he shows enthusiasm about his attempt to pursue his goals. It brings out a person who is excited about seeing his or her goal become a reality.

In 2011, I had the opportunity to see Zig Ziglar at the Toyota Center in Houston, Texas. He stood there on stage at the age of eighty-four with is daughter, who was there to keep him focused. On occasion, he had wandered off topic from a subject he was speaking about. Therefore, she would always bring him back to the point when he had a speaking engagement.

Now there is a man who still has fun doing what he really enjoys. Zig Ziglar has been giving motivational speeches and writing book for several years. In his book *See You at the Top*, he suggests that we reverse the way we get out of bed in the morning if we want to develop enthusiasm and the right mental attitude about all life has to offer. He claims that most people moan a bit, slap their faces, and think, *Oh no, don't tell me it's time to get up already. I feel like I just lay down.*

He believes there is a better way to start your day. Tomorrow morning when the alarm clock goes off, reach over and shut it off. Then immediately sit straight up in bed, clap your hands, and say, "Oh boy. It's a great day to get out and face the world." If you live to be a hundred, you will never tell a bigger one than that. However, let me emphasize something important. You're up, and that's where you wanted to be when you set the alarm. You're taking control of your attitude.

Ziglar stresses that when you start the day with a lot of excitement and enthusiasm, you're on target, according to the Bible. Psalm 118:24

says, "This is the day which the Lord has made. I will rejoice and be glad in it."

If you take the suggestion of Ziglar, it will get you going and laughing at yourself in the morning. The enthusiasm you create will develop an attitude that causes you to look for a fun and joyous day. This is one way to start your day as a way to be glad and have fun as you move closer to you goal.

Once you have identified the things you want in life, made them your goals, and started on your journey to accomplish them, do not forget to keep a *fun* attitude about it. Really enjoy the moment.

Buckled down at thirty thousand feet on a two-hour flight, one may overlook the joy and pleasantry that is around you. While the plane was flying above the clouds toward a warmer destination, we began to watch the flight attendants as they did their job. They seemed to be enjoying themselves. We could say that they were focused on their job and having fun in the present moment.

Do me a favor. Yes, I know this is somewhat awkward to request this simple task at this time. But right here, right now, I want you to smile. No, I mean really smile and then look around to see if anyone is looking. I wouldn't want anyone to think you are crazy. Now you would have to admit that made you feel refreshed and good inside and out. Right? Right.

See, that is the secret. If you could keep that feeling every day of your life through all circumstances, it would be great. That is why this formula was developed. I have called it the "forever formula." When you apply this formula to situations that have cause you to be depressed and stressed, I believe it will encourage you to try to maintain that happy feeling inside. Plus, this technique will allow you to refocus on the wonderful journey on which you have embarked.

There are many ways that a person can be enlightened. Nevertheless, since you are reading this book and writing down the ideas that come in your mind, you are starting to think about all the possibilities that you would like to pursue. When you become excited all over again, you once again become passionate about your projects and endeavors. This new rejuvenation of passion in your soul reignites the fires of your heart.

This fun attitude is something you need to keep; it will allow you to flush out all the unnecessary negative energy that you may encounter each and every day.

You have probably heard people say that they love their jobs. If the person is sincere about this statement, then he or she is probably turning out good quality work and is probably a pleasure to be around. When people see you as a fun person to be around, they are more willing to help you if you need it.

As I come to the ending of this book about success principles, I liken it to the pilot making the announcement that we have permission to land.

The plane began to lower its wheels for landing, and as he got closer to the runway, there was a big sense of relief. Excited about finally reaching the destination, I immediately started thinking about the next goal.

When you finally reach your goal, you need to celebrate. Because the minute after you reach it, there will be more goals to maintain your original one.

Focus on Your Goal

Write your main goal at the bottom of this chart and then list the steps it will take to reach this milestone at the beginning of this chart.

Steps to Reach Your Goal

1.

2.

3.

4.

5.

Steps to Reach Your Secondary Goal

1.

2.

3.

4.

5.

Short-Range Goal Target Date: _____

Long-Range Goal Target Date: _____

About the Author

He is a person you can trust and a true friend to those who know him. He has felt the pain of disappointment, deception, lies, and heartache. He has tasted the sweet joy of victory, laughter, and happiness. His focus is to make life processes simple but great.

Printed in the United States
By Bookmasters